# Tracing
# Derry - Londonderry
# Roots

*By*
**Brian Mitchell**

**CLEARFIELD**

Reprinted for Clearfield Company by
Genealogical Publishing Company
Baltimore, Maryland
2014

ISBN 978-0-8063-5695-2

# Table of Contents

This section examines each of the nine major record sources and where they can be accessed locally, nationally and on the internet.

Local libraries: Derry Central Library
Coleraine Library
The Mellon Centre for Migration Studies at Ulster American Folk Park
Foyle Family History Centre
Derry City Council: Archive and Genealogy Service

## The Major Record Offices

General Register Office, Dublin and Roscommon
General Register Office Northern Ireland, Belfast
National Archives of Ireland, Dublin
National Library of Ireland, Dublin
Public Record Office of Northern Ireland, Belfast

**List of Illustrations**

## Introduction

People care deeply about who they are and where they come from; in Ireland, place and kin hold a very strong emotional bond. It is said that when Amelia Earhart (the first woman to fly solo across the Atlantic from Harbour Grace, Newfoundland to Londonderry) landed, on Saturday 21 May 1932, in front of Dan McCallion's cottage, she asked: "Where am I?" An astonished Dan McCallion, who was out herding his cattle, replied: "In Gallagher's Pasture".

The purpose of this small book is quite simply to assist anyone, local people and visitors alike, research their family history in the city and county of Londonderry (also known as Derry). Derry and Londonderry refer to the same place; the royal charter of James I officially created the city of Londonderry and the county of Londonderry on 29 March 1613.

It is true that during the civil war the shelling of the Four Courts, Dublin on 28 June 1922 resulted in a fire and the destruction of many important historical documents, including many Church of Ireland registers, wills and 19th century census returns. A primary aim of this book, however, is to dispel the widely held notion that most records of genealogical interest for Derry were destroyed; they weren't.

Major record sources such as civil registers of births, marriages and deaths and the registers of Roman Catholic parishes and Presbyterian congregations were not destroyed in this fire. Furthermore, copies, transcripts and abstracts of many wills and Church of Ireland registers, together with the existence of census substitutes, have lessened the impact of the Four Courts' fire.

There are two essential aspects to Irish family history research: the search for birth, marriage and death events; and an examination of census returns and census substitutes for the locality (i.e. townland and parish) in which your ancestor resided.

I believe that initiating research into your Derry ancestry is quite straightforward; in my opinion, there are nine major record sources to examine. The sources being:

- Civil registers of births, marriages and deaths
- Church registers of baptisms, marriages and burials
- Gravestone inscriptions
- Wills
- 1901 and 1911 Census returns
- Mid-19th century Griffith's Valuation
- Early-19th century Tithe Applotment Books
- 1831 Census
- Pre-1800 Census substitutes

This book will examine each of these sources and where they can be found. These sources should be searched before you consider further research options.

These sources can be variously examined at three locations: in local record offices; in national repositories in Belfast and Dublin; and in an expanding range of databases, many of which can be accessed on the internet.

An overview of local and national archives of relevance to those researching their Derry~Londonderry roots, with contact details and short descriptions of record sources held, are recorded in glossaries at the back of the book. Always refer to the glossaries when seeking additional information on any record office mentioned in the main body of this book.

## Background to Derry Genealogy

### Derry or Londonderry?

As the terms Derry and Londonderry cause so much confusion to family historians from outside Ireland, it is necessary to provide a brief history.

By tradition, in 546 AD, the church of Doire Calgach, "the oak wood of Calgach", was founded by St Columcille, also known as St Columba, on the crest of a small, wooded hill on the west bank of the River Foyle. The original church of hewn oak, thatched with reeds, was located where St Augustine's Church stands today. For the next one thousand years Derry was a monastic centre of some importance.

The city of Londonderry, a settlement funded by the city of London, was established, on the island of Derry, by royal charter of James I on 29 March 1613. By 1619 the city was completely enclosed within a stone wall, 24 feet high and 18 feet thick. This walled city assumed a pivotal role in safeguarding the settlement of 17th century English and Scottish planters as its walls repulsed Sieges in 1641, 1649 and 1689.

The charter of 1613 also defined and established a new county which was also called Londonderry. The new County of Londonderry had been enlarged, and consisted of the County of Coleraine, the heavily wooded Barony of Loughinsholin in Tyrone, the City and Liberties of Londonderry on the Donegal side of the River Foyle, and the Town and Liberties of Coleraine on the Antrim side of the River Bann.

Today, it is a matter of personal preference to refer to the city and county as either Derry or Londonderry. For example, the *Londonderry Journal*, established on 3 June 1772, continued as the *Derry Journal* from 22 March 1880.

## Surnames

Surnames, or inherited family names, are the building blocks of genealogy; without them, it would be impossible to trace our ancestors back through the generations. Irish surnames can provide clues and insight into the origins of your family history as, in many cases, they offer an authentic link between history, location and identity.

Surnames, as they are very much connected to place in Ireland, are an integral part of Irish identity and family history. Surnames of Gaelic Irish origin frequently confirm membership of a sept. It was assumed that members of an Irish sept had a common tribal ancestor. Thus, even today, Gaelic Irish surnames are still very dominant and numerous in the very localities where their names originated. For example, the surname McCloskey both originates and predominates today in the Dungiven area of County Derry.

Not only was County Derry the last stronghold of powerful Gaelic tribes, it also became home to many settlers from England and, in particular, Scotland during the Plantation of Ulster in the 17th century. Thus Derry was home to many emigrants, of Gaelic Irish, Gaelic Scottish, Lowland Scottish and English origins, who departed, over a period of three centuries, for new lives in North America, Great Britain and Australasia.

By examining surname reference books or by using the "Surname search" facility on the Irish Ancestors website at www.irishtimes.com/ancestor, you can build up a picture of the location and history of Irish surnames.

You will find that in the context of Irish historical records there are many spelling variations of the same name. There is no doubt that the process of anglicisation has obscured the origins of many Irish surnames. From the 17th century Gaelic surnames of Irish and Scottish origin were translated, and in many cases mistranslated, into English; others were changed to similar-sounding English names. Family names of Gaelic origin were further disguised in the 18th century by discarding the prefix Mac, Mc and O.

Thus, in conducting family history research you should be aware of the possibility of different spellings of the same surname. For example, Doherty can also be written, to name but a few, as Dogherty, Dougherty, Docherty, O Dochartaigh, O'Doagharty, O'Dogherty and O'Doherty in record sources; and Rosborough as Rosborrow, Rossborough, Rossboro, Roxborough, Roxbrough and Roxberry.

**Place**

The key to unlocking Irish family history origins is the knowledge of place. In tracing your roots in Derry the most important piece of information to treasure, to be gleaned from either family folklore or record sources, is any information as to a place of origin of your ancestors.

John Steinbeck, Nobel prize-winning author who visited Derry in August 1952 knew exactly where his roots lay: "We were looking for a place called Mulkeraugh. You can spell it half a dozen ways and it isn't on any map. I knew from half-memory that it was near to Ballykelly, which is near to Limavady, and I knew that from Mulkeraugh you could look across the lough to the hills of Donegal." Full details of Steinbeck's eventful trip to Ireland were recorded in his article "I Go Back To Ireland" which was published in *Collier's Magazine* of 31 January 1953 together with four photographs by his wife Elaine.

Samuel Hamilton, the maternal grandfather of John Steinbeck, was born at Mulkeeragh on 7 October 1830. The townland of Mulkeeragh, 335 acres in size, can be found just to the south-east of the village of Ballykelly.

From a family historian's perspective the most effective way to view Derry is as a county which is subdivided into parishes and which in turn are subdivided into townlands. County Derry, prior to the 20th century, was administered by 46 civil parishes which contained 1248 townlands, with an average size of 408 acres.

As many records of genealogical value were compiled on a parish basis it means that realistic genealogical research, in the absence of indexes and databases, requires knowledge of the parish in which your ancestor lived. If sources are not indexed you then need to know where your ancestor lived before you can begin to select appropriate records to search.

Identification of the ancestral home in County Derry effectively means identifying the townland your ancestor lived in. The townland is the smallest and most ancient of Irish land divisions. The townland was named at an early period, and it usually referred to a very identifiable landmark in the local area such as a mountain, a bog, an oak forest, a village, a fort or a church.

Townlands vary greatly in area as their size was generally based on the fertility of the land. In Faughanvale Parish, which contains 66 townlands, the fertile lowland townland of Muff is some 318 acres in size, while Killywool which extends into the Loughermore Hills contains 1,471 acres. The townland was loosely based on the ancient Irish land measure called the ballyboe, which means cow townland. As a ballyboe was based on the area that could support a fixed number of cattle, it is not surprising that their size varied depending on land quality.

The "Placenames" option at www.irishtimes.com/ancestor allows you to locate the civil parish and poor law union locations of all of Derry's townlands. Furthermore, civil parish locations, and their associated townlands, can be located at www.irishtimes.com/ancestor/browse/counties/civilmaps/index. cfm by selecting Derry on the map of Ireland.

# THE PARISHES OF COUNTY LONDONDERRY

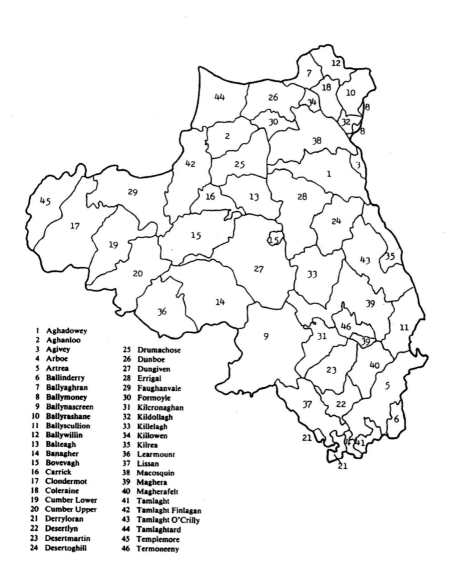

1 Aghadowey
2 Aghanloo
3 Agivey
4 Arboe
5 Artrea
6 Ballinderry
7 Ballyaghran
8 Ballymoney
9 Ballynascreen
10 Ballyrashane
11 Ballyscullion
12 Ballywillin
13 Balteagh
14 Banagher
15 Bovevagh
16 Carrick
17 Clondermot
18 Coleraine
19 Cumber Lower
20 Cumber Upper
21 Derryloran
22 Desertlyn
23 Desertmartin
24 Desertoghill

25 Drumachose
26 Dunboe
27 Dungiven
28 Errigal
29 Faughanvale
30 Formoyle
31 Kilcronaghan
32 Kildollagh
33 Killelagh
34 Killowen
35 Kilrea
36 Learmount
37 Lissan
38 Macosquin
39 Maghera
40 Magherafelt
41 Tamlaght
42 Tamlaght Finlagan
43 Tamlaght O'Crilly
44 Tamlaghtard
45 Templemore
46 Termoneeny

THE TOWNLANDS OF FAUGHANVALE PARISH

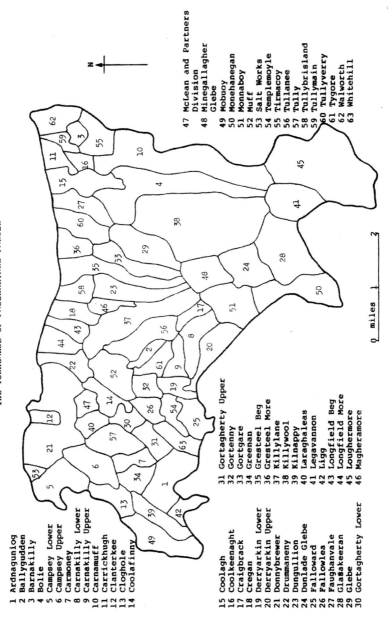

N

0 miles 1 2

1 Ardnaguniog
2 Ballygudden
3 Barnakilly
4 Bolie
5 Campsey Lower
6 Campsey Upper
7 Carmoney
8 Carnakilly Lower
9 Carnakilly Upper
10 Carnamuff
11 Carrickhugh
12 Clanterkee
13 Cloghole
14 Coolafinny

15 Coolagh
16 Coolkeenaght
17 Craigbrack
18 Cregan
19 Derryarkin Lower
20 Derryarkin Upper
21 Donnybrewer
22 Drummaneny
23 Dungullion
24 Dunlade Glebe
25 Fallowlea
26 Faughanvale
27 Glack
28 Glasakeeran
29 Glebe
30 Gortagherty Lower

31 Gortagherty Upper
32 Gortenny
33 Gortgare
34 Greenan
35 Gresteel Beg
36 Gresteel More
37 Killylane
38 Killywool
39 Kilnappy
40 Laraghaleas
41 Legavannon
42 Ligg
43 Longfield Beg
44 Longfield More
45 Loughermore
46 Magheramore

47 McLean and Partners Division
48 Minegallagher Glebe
49 Mobuoy
50 Monehanegan
51 Monnaboy
52 Muff
53 Salt Works
54 Templemoyle
55 Tirmacoy
56 Tullanee
57 Tully
58 Tullybrisland
59 Tullymain
60 Tullyverry
61 Tygore
62 Walworth
63 Whitehill

To gain insight into the economic and social landscape of 19th century Ireland you can consult *A Topographical Dictionary of Ireland,* published in 1837, by Samuel Lewis. Arranged in alphabetical order by place this dictionary provides an overview of the geography and history of Ireland's villages, parishes and towns, as they existed at the time of publication (1837). This book can now be viewed online at http://www.libraryireland.com/topog/placeindex.php, by selecting an initial letter; for example 'T' if you wish to view information on Tamlaghtard (also known as Magilligan) parish.

**Emigration Port and Passenger Lists**

From the early 1700s to the onset of the Second World War in 1939, when the last transatlantic steamer sailed from the port, Derry was one of the principal emigration ports in Ireland.

Between 1717 and the War of American Independence, 250,000 Scots-Irish (i.e. descendants of 17th century Scottish planters) emigrated through the ports of Belfast, Derry, Newry, Larne and Portrush for the British Colonies in North America. The Ulster-Scots tended to enter America through Philadelphia and then headed for the frontier. It is estimated that in 1771 and 1772, during a slump in the linen trade, 17,150 emigrants departed on 61 ships from the five principal ports of the north of Ireland. Twenty-two of these ships, of which 16 were destined for Philadelphia, carrying 6,300 emigrants or 36% of the total, left from Derry. Belfast, the next largest emigration port, carried 4,200 emigrants or 26% of the total.

Derry's importance as an emigration port increased throughout the 19th century. It was a profitable trade. Merchants in Derry soon became ship-owners as opposed to agents for American and British companies. An outward cargo of emigrants, a homeward cargo of timber, flaxseed or grain, together with two voyages per year, one in spring and one in the autumn, ensured a sizeable profit. By 1833 seven merchants in the city owned fifteen vessels, all engaged in the North American trade; and, by the 1850s, two local companies, J & J Cooke and William McCorkell & Co, had built up sizeable shipping fleets.

Prior to the 1860s, and the establishment of a railway network in Ireland, the port of Derry served as the emigration port for Counties Derry, Donegal and Tyrone. Saint John (New Brunswick) and Quebec in Canada, and New York and Philadelphia in USA were the destination ports for these emigrants. In 1847, 12,385 emigrants, 41% of them carried by local merchants J & J Cooke, sailed from Derry in sailing ships.

By the 1870s sailing ships could no longer compete with the speed, comfort and reliability of the transatlantic passenger steamers. In 1873 the *Minnehaha,* the flagship of William McCorkell & Co, which was known in New York as "the green yacht from Derry", made the last transatlantic passenger voyage by a Derry-owned ship.

From 1865 right through to 1939 liners anchored at Moville in the deeper waters of Lough Foyle, some 18 miles downstream from Derry. Emigrants were now carried from Derry quay in paddle tenders to connect with the ocean-going liners of the Anchor Line of Glasgow and of the Allan Line and Dominion Line of Liverpool. In 1883, 15,000 people left through Derry, by steamship, for Canada and the USA.

By the turn of the 20th century Derry was the major emigration port for the northern half of Ireland, with emigrants being brought to Derry quay by an extensive rail network.

Official passenger departure lists (which record UK addresses from 1922) recording emigrants who sailed from Derry to Canada and USA exist from 1890 and these can now be searched online at www.ancestorsonboard.com by name, port, ship and date. For example, this database reveals that 134 passengers with the surname Doherty sailed on the *City of Rome,* an Anchor Line ship, from Derry to New York between 1891 and 1901 inclusive.

Passenger departure lists naming Derry emigrants have been extracted from four different sources for the years 1803-1806, 1833-1839 and 1847-1871, and published in three books by the Genealogical Publishing Company. The details are:

- *Irish Passenger Lists, 1803 – 1806: Lists of Passengers Sailing from Ireland to America Extracted from the Hardwicke Papers.*
- *Irish Emigration Lists, 1833 – 1839: Lists of Emigrants Extracted from the Ordnance Survey Memoirs for Counties Londonderry and Antrim.*
- *Irish Passenger Lists, 1847 – 1871: Lists of Passengers Sailing from Londonderry to America on Ships of the J. & J. Cooke Line and the McCorkell Line.*

Derry Central Library and Derry Genealogy Centre hold copies of these books. Furthermore, indexes and scanned images of these three books are also included in Family Tree Maker's CD – *Irish Immigrants to North America* – which contains 10 volumes of published Irish passenger lists, naming approximately 60,000 immigrants, the earliest list dating from 1735, the latest 1871.

As a general rule, prior to 1890, you are more likely to identify passengers at the port of arrival as opposed to the port of departure. You can now access, for free, passenger arrival records to US ports, at any branch library in Northern Ireland, by searching 'Ancestry Library Edition' on the Northern Ireland Library Service's website www.librariesni.org.uk.

One of the most significant databases available to library users (or by subscription to www.ancestry.com) is the 'US Immigration Collection' which contains indexes to passenger lists of ships arriving from foreign ports to Boston from 1820 to 1943 (3.8 million immigrants), Philadelphia, 1800 to 1945 (1.6 million), and New York, 1820 to 1957 (83 million). Information contained in the index includes: given name, surname, age, gender, ethnicity, nationality or last country of permanent residence, destination, arrival date, port of arrival, port of departure and ship name. Furthermore, the names found in the index are linked to actual images of the passenger lists.

The 'US Immigration Collection' also names 16.3 million passengers arriving in the UK (from foreign ports outside of Europe) between 1878 and 1960; 8.4 million 'unassisted' immigrants to New South Wales, Australia from 1826 to 1922 and 450,000 'assisted' immigrants to New South Wales from 1828-1896; and 7.3 million passengers arriving at Canadian ports between 1865 and 1935.

### Genetic Genealogy: The Future?

Genetic genealogy has been described as "the newest and most exciting addition to genealogy research". Businesses (such as Oxford Ancestors at www.oxfordancestors.com) and projects (such as Ulster Heritage's DNA Ancestry Project at www.ulsterheritage.com) have been established in recent years to assist researchers discover their ancestral roots through DNA connections.

DNA is the genetic material within our cells that is handed down from generation to generation. Within it is written not only our personal history, but the history of the whole human race. The human genetic code, or genome, is 99.9% identical throughout the world. What's left is the DNA responsible for our individual differences. A random, harmless mutation can occur which is then passed down to all of that person's descendants. Generations later, finding that same mutation, or marker, in two people's DNA indicate that they share the same ancestor. By comparing markers in many different populations, scientists can trace their ancestral connections.

These minute changes in genetic material are preserved in your mitochondrial DNA (mtDNA) which is passed down intact from mother to child and in the Y chromosome (yDNA) which travels from father to son (yDNA signatures are inherited, in the majority of cases, with surname over time). These genes pass from generation to generation and they don't change except by a slow process of mutation. By comparing DNA markers you can construct probability statistics as to what extent two people share a common ancestor; while the degree of difference in markers is an indication of how long ago they shared a common ancestor.

Geneticists at Trinity College, Dublin claim that as many as 1 in 5 people in North West Ireland are descended from a common ancestor who "was likely to have lived about 1,700 years ago". This concentration in the north-west, together with the time factor; pointed, in the eyes of the researchers at Trinity College, to the Ui Neill dynasty. Ui Neill means 'descendants of Niall'; Niall being Niall of the Nine Hostages, High King of Ireland from 379 to 405 AD.

By tradition two of Niall's sons, Conall Gulban and Eoghan, were the paternal ancestors of the major Gaelic families of Counties Derry, Donegal and Tyrone. Those tracing descent from Eoghan include: Brolly, Carlin, Devlin, Donnelly, Duddy, Duffy, Farren, Gormley, Hegarty, McCloskey, McLaughlin, Mellon, Mullen, O'Hagan, O'Kane, O'Neill, Quinn and Toner. From Conall Gulban: Doherty, Friel, Gallagher, McCafferty, McDaid, McDevitt and O'Donnell.

## First Steps

## Family Reminiscences and Family Papers

The first, and perhaps the most crucial, step in compiling your family tree is probably the one many people neglect: namely, the quizzing of relations and family friends.

Parents, grandparents, uncles and aunts should all be questioned. Names, dates, places of birth and any anecdotes, no matter how unlikely or inaccurate you might think them to be, associated with all branches of your family tree should be recorded. In genealogy, you never know when a piece of information that seemed irrelevant, might, on reflection, suggest a line of inquiry.

Family memories and knowledge should not be underestimated. There are many instances where family folklore, passed down through the generations, extends beyond what is written in historical records or captured in databases.

Historical research and story telling should not be separated; they are both crucial in any attempt to construct your family history. Yes, as family historians we are seeking facts to the origins of our ancestry but, let's be honest, it's the anecdotes and stories that capture our imagination and certainly the interest of others. The information and anecdotes relatives can provide help bring the family tree to life, as well as providing much-needed clues for its construction. The oral traditions within the family circle are, therefore, of immense interest and value.

John Steinbeck, reminiscing in *Collier's Magazine* (31 January 1953) about the roots of his mother, Olive Hamilton, wrote: "I guess the people of my family thought of Ireland as a green paradise, mother of heroes, where golden people sprang full-flowered from the sod. I don't remember my mother actually telling me these things, but she must have given me such an impression of delight. Only kings and heroes came from this Holy Island, and at the very top of the glittering pyramid was our family, the Hamiltons."

In addition to oral tradition, a search should be made through family papers to unearth old photographs, newspaper clippings with perhaps an obituary, letters, or even a family bible with its own family tree within. You never know until you look, what useful information may be lurking in the back of a cupboard or hiding in a box in the attic.

**Record Your Information**

It is important to record and organise the information you gather about your family history. The simplest method is to record birth, marriage and death details of direct line ancestors, i.e. parents, grandparents and great grandparents, on a purpose-designed pedigree chart. Information that is unknown is simply left blank, thus highlighting those areas where further research is needed.

A large selection of family tree charts, in many styles and degrees of complexity, on which to begin recording your family history can also be downloaded and printed, for free, on the internet at www.misbach.org, by selecting 'free PDF Charts.'
Purpose-designed pedigree charts usually offer no space for detailing brothers and sisters of direct line ancestors and their descendants. The solution, therefore, is quite simply to draw your own family chart in which there are no limitations to size. A further advantage of such a chart is that you choose what families to highlight.

The conventions in drawing up your own family chart are straighforward. Start at the top of the page with the ancestor whose descendants you want to record and link him to his wife with the recognised marriage symbol of =. From this marriage symbol, draw a vertical line to join a horizontal line whose length is determined by the number of children attached to it by other short vertical lines. The same procedure is followed for any other marriages amongst these children. Children should be listed in order of birth, but in some circumstances it is an advantage to change the order so as to fit the requirements of your chart design. The following standard symbols and abbreviations should be used: b. for born, c. about, m. married, d. died, ? if uncertain of accuracy of information, and blank spaces for information which is not yet known.

If possible, always record people of the same generation on the same level. For example, current generation at level 1, parents' details at level 2, grandparents at level 3, great-grandparents at level 4 and so on.

An example of such a chart has been drawn up to present the family history of the Hasty family of Kilrea, County Derry.

With this type of family chart, it is perhaps best to draw up a rough draft to ensure all descendants you want to include can be accommodated, as such charts lose their clarity if you continually add to them.

With family information gathered and then recorded in family tree charts, you are now ready to begin research through written historical sources which are held in a variety of local and national record offices. Many of these sources can also be accessed in a growing number of databases.

**Family Tree of Hasty Family of Kilrea, County Londonderry**

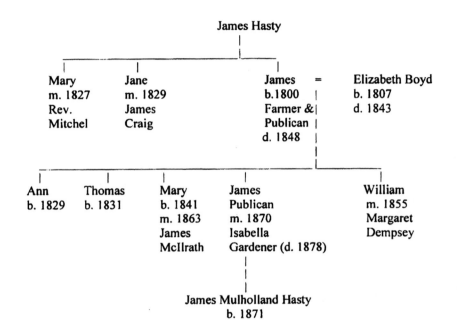

James Hasty

| Mary | Jane | James = Elizabeth Boyd |
| m. 1827 | m. 1829 | b.1800   b. 1807 |
| Rev. | James | Farmer & d. 1843 |
| Mitchel | Craig | Publican |
|  |  | d. 1848 |

| Ann | Thomas | Mary | James | William |
| b. 1829 | b. 1831 | b. 1841 | Publican | m. 1855 |
|  |  | m. 1863 | m. 1870 | Margaret |
|  |  | James | Isabella | Dempsey |
|  |  | McIlrath | Gardener (d. 1878) |

James Mulholland Hasty
b. 1871

**The Main Record Sources**

In this section I will detail the major Irish record sources in terms of what information they contain, their limitations, where they can be found and how they can be accessed.

**Civil Registers of Births, Marriages and Deaths**

Civil registration in Ireland of births, deaths and Roman Catholic marriages began on 1st January 1864 while Protestant marriages were subject to registration from 1st April 1845. For the purpose of civil registration, Ireland was divided into about 800 registrar districts, which were grouped into 140 poor law unions. Books recording births, marriages and deaths were kept in each local registrar district, and a consolidated name index, with limited information, was then compiled at national level.

The detail included in birth, marriage and death registers, together with their associated indexes, help to make this source an ideal starting point in researching Derry ancestors.

A civil **birth** entry records the name, date of birth and place of birth of the child together with the father's name, occupation and residence, and the mother's name and maiden name.

A civil **marriage** entry gives the date and place of marriage and the names, ages, occupations and residences of the bride and groom together with the names and occupations of their fathers and the names of two witnesses.

A civil **death** entry supplies the deceased's name, age, occupation, date of death, place of death and cause of death.

Civil birth, marriage and death registers are indexed; the early indexes were compiled annually while the later ones (from 1878) were arranged by quarter year. They are arranged in alphabetical order by surname and then by Christian name.

## Civil Register of Births

District of: **Articlave**
Union of: **Coleraine**
County of: **Londonderry**
Book Number: **2**
Entry Number: **366**

Birth Date: **12 March 1870**
Birth Place: **Liffock**

| Name (if any) | Sex | Name and Surname and Dwelling-place of Father | Name and Surname and Maiden Surname of Mother | Rank or Profession of Father | Signature, Qualification and Residence of Informant | When Registered |
|---|---|---|---|---|---|---|
| Mary | Female | William Loughery, Liffock | Jane Loughery *formerly* Rose | Labourer | Mary Rose (X her mark), present at Birth, Liffock | 28 March 1870 |

# Civil Register of Marriages

Registrar's District: **Londonderry**
County: **Londonderry**
Place of Worship: **Glendermott Parish Church**
Register: **3**
Number: **102**

Marriage solemnized at **The Parish Church** in the **Parish of Glendermott** in the **County Londonderry**

When Married: **12 July 1875**

| Name and Surname | Age | Condition | Rank or Profession | Residence at the Time of Marriage | Father's Name and Surname | Rank or Profession of Father |
|---|---|---|---|---|---|---|
| William Cowan | Full | Bachelor | Labourer | Drumahoe | William Cowan | Labourer |
| Mary Jane Brown | Full | Spinster | | Mill Street | John Brown | Labourer |

Married in the Parish Church according to the Rites and Ceremonies of the Church of Ireland, by licence by me,

*D Babington*

This Marriage was solemnized between us, *William* (X his mark) *Cowan* and *Mary Jane Browne*

in the Presence of us, *Bella Brown* and *William Campbell*

# Civil Register of Deaths

District of: **Eglinton**
Union of: **Londonderry**
County of: **Londonderry**
Book Number: **3**
Entry Number: **334**

Death Date: **22 January 1877**
Place of Death: **Ballyowen, Glendermott**

| Name and Surname | Sex | Condition | Age last Birthday | Rank, profession or occupation | Certified Cause of Death | Signature, Qualification and Residence of Informant | When Registered |
|---|---|---|---|---|---|---|---|
| John Browne | Male | Married | 45 years | Labourer | Heart Disease | George Duddy (X his mark), present at death, Ballyowen | 3 February 1877 |

In the time period 1864 to 1902 and 1928 to 1966 the indexes to births, marriages and deaths list: year (quarter year from 1878) of registration of the event; name; the poor law union in which the event was registered; and the volume and page number in which the event will be found. The indexes for 1903 to 1927 provide additional information such as the date of the event; mother's maiden name in birth indexes; partner's surname in marriage indexes; and age and marital condition of deceased in death indexes.

It is clear that the indexes, especially prior to 1902, give limited information. A birth or death, for example, will be hard to identify without a fairly clear idea of when and where it happened. Furthermore the only guidance to an address in the indexes is the poor law union in which the event was registered. This, therefore, means that the only address information provided in the national indexes to birth, marriage or death events in County Derry are the five poor law union names of Ballymoney, Coleraine, Londonderry, Newtownlimavady (now known as Limavady) and Magherafelt.

On the other hand as the marriage indexes will list both parties (in their appropriate alphabetical placing), there is a cross-referencing system which may enable the identification of a marriage in the absence of both an address and date.

The national indexes to civil birth, marriage and death events, prior to 1922, for County Derry can be examined, on payment of the appropriate search fees, at two offices:

The General Register Office, Oxford House, 49-55 Chichester Street, Belfast, BT1 4HL, Northern Ireland

The General Register Office, Family History Research Facility, Werburgh Street, Dublin 2, Ireland

As of 31 March 2014 you can search and view records, by purchasing credits, of births (over 100 years old), marriages (over 75 years old) and deaths (over 50 years old) for Northern Ireland (i.e. Counties Antrim, Armagh, Down, Fermanagh, Londonderry and Tyrone) on the website of the General Register Office of Northern Ireland (www.nidirect.gov.uk/gro).

You can also search, at no charge, the pre-1922 civil registration indexes for Derry on the website of the Church of Jesus Christ of Latter-Day Saints at www.familysearch.org (by selecting 'Search' tab and clicking on 'United Kingdom and Ireland' from 'Browse by Location', and then selecting from country list, which is in alphabetical order, 'Ireland, Civil Registration Indexes, 1845-1958'). Furthermore, at their local Family History Centre on the Racecourse Road, Derry you can view, for free, microfilm copies of the following civil registers for all Ireland: Births from 1864 to 1881 (first quarter); Marriages 1845 to1870; and Deaths 1864 to 1870.

The database of Derry Genealogy Centre contains full transcriptions of all pre-1922 civil marriage registers and the bulk of pre-1922 civil birth registers for the city and county of Derry. As this database was created from the original local registers, and captured all information, it offers much greater flexibility in searching for birth and marriage events than the existing national indexes. This database can now be accessed online at www.derry.rootsireland.ie.

**Church Registers of Baptisms, Marriages and Burials**

Prior to the commencement of civil registration of births, marriages and deaths in Ireland, family history researchers usually rely on baptismal, marriage and burial registers kept by churches to confirm birth, marriage and death details of ancestors.

A **baptism** entry can provide the name of the child; date of baptism; date of birth; parents' names including maiden name of mother; parents' address (by townland); occupation; and names of sponsors (particularly in Roman Catholic registers).

A **marriage** entry can provide the names of the bride and groom; their places of residence; date of marriage; parents' names; and names of witnesses.

A **burial** entry can provide the name and residence of the deceased; burial date and place; age of the deceased. In the case of children, the names of parents may be included.

Church registers, like civil registers, can clearly supply enough information to build and confirm family linkages. However, access to church registers, in the absence of indexes and databases, is gained through knowledge of the parish address and religious denomination of an ancestor. Dates of commencement and quality of information in church registers vary from parish to parish and from denomination to denomination.

Church of Ireland parishes normally conform to the civil parish, though Roman Catholic parishes do not, as they are generally larger. The Roman Catholic Church, owing to the Reformation of the sixteenth century, had to adapt itself to a new structure centred on towns and villages. The Presbyterian church doesn't have a parish structure, with the congregations generally forming where there was sufficient demand from local Presbyterian families.

Church registers should always be examined once you know the parish location and religious denomination of your ancestor. In the 19th century, 28 Roman Catholic parishes, 53 Church of Ireland parishes, 65 Presbyterian Congregations and 4 Methodist circuits served the population of County Derry. Public Record Office of Northern Ireland's *Guide To Church Records* which lists, in alphabetical order by civil parish, church registers of all denominations is a useful source for identifying the commencement dates of most of Derry's church registers.

# THE ROMAN CATHOLIC PARISHES
# OF COUNTY LONDONDERRY

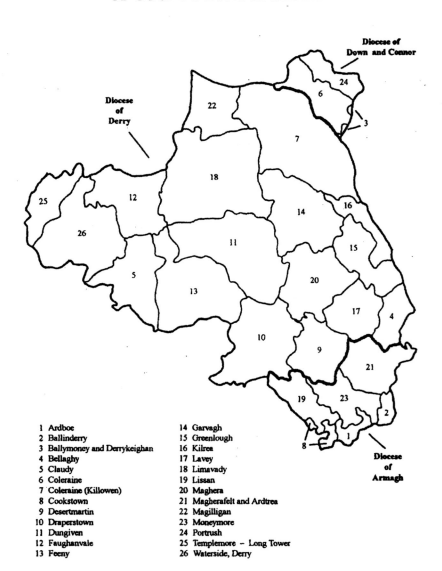

| | |
|---|---|
| 1 Ardboe | 14 Garvagh |
| 2 Ballinderry | 15 Greenlough |
| 3 Ballymoney and Derrykeighan | 16 Kilrea |
| 4 Bellaghy | 17 Lavey |
| 5 Claudy | 18 Limavady |
| 6 Coleraine | 19 Lissan |
| 7 Coleraine (Killowen) | 20 Maghera |
| 8 Cookstown | 21 Magherafelt and Ardtrea |
| 9 Desertmartin | 22 Magilligan |
| 10 Draperstown | 23 Moneymore |
| 11 Dungiven | 24 Portrush |
| 12 Faughanvale | 25 Templemore – Long Tower |
| 13 Feeny | 26 Waterside, Derry |

# THE PRESBYTERIAN CONGREGATIONS
## OF COUNTY LONDONDERRY

1 Aghadowey
2 Ballyarnett
3 Ballygoney
4 Ballykelly
5 Ballylintagh
6 Ballyrashane
7 Ballywillin
8 Balteagh
9 Banagher
10 Bellaghy 1st and 2nd
11 Boveedy
12 Bovevagh

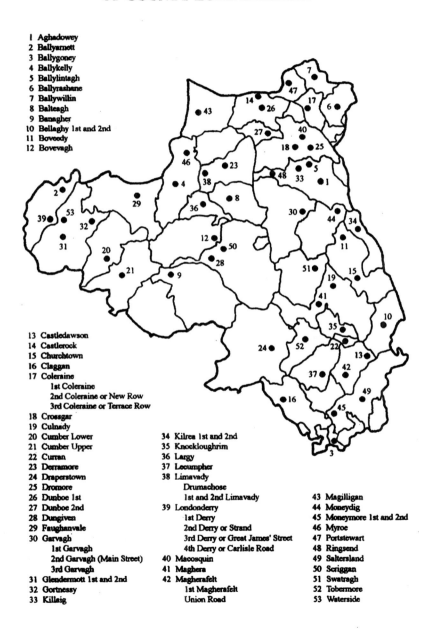

13 Castledawson
14 Castlerock
15 Churchtown
16 Claggan
17 Coleraine
    1st Coleraine
    2nd Coleraine or New Row
    3rd Coleraine or Terrace Row
18 Crossgar
19 Culnady
20 Cumber Lower
21 Cumber Upper
22 Curran
23 Derramore
24 Draperstown
25 Dromore
26 Dunboe 1st
27 Dunboe 2nd
28 Dungiven
29 Faughanvale
30 Garvagh
    1st Garvagh
    2nd Garvagh (Main Street)
    3rd Garvagh
31 Glendermott 1st and 2nd
32 Gortnessy
33 Killaig

34 Kilrea 1st and 2nd
35 Knockloughrim
36 Largy
37 Lecumpher
38 Limavady
    Drumachose
    1st and 2nd Limavady
39 Londonderry
    1st Derry
    2nd Derry or Strand
    3rd Derry or Great James' Street
    4th Derry or Carlisle Road
40 Macosquin
41 Maghera
42 Magherafelt
    1st Magherafelt
    Union Road

43 Magilligan
44 Moneydig
45 Moneymore 1st and 2nd
46 Myroe
47 Portstewart
48 Ringsend
49 Saltersland
50 Scriggan
51 Swatragh
52 Tobermore
53 Waterside

This guide can also be accessed on their website (www.proni.gov.uk) by selecting 'online guides.'

Microfilm copies of the majority of church registers of all denominations for County Derry can be examined in either the Public Record Office of Northern Ireland in Belfast or in Coleraine Library. Furthermore, the National Library of Ireland in Dublin holds microfilm copy of pre-1880 registers for Roman Catholic parishes of County Derry.

There is no national index to church registers. To date, in Ireland, only the county-based genealogical research centres have attempted any large scale, systematic indexing of church registers in their localities. County Derry is fortunate in this regard as a very significant collection of 85 church registers (26 Roman Catholic, 24 Church of Ireland and 35 Presbyterian) were computerised by Derry Genealogy Centre; the details in these baptismal, marriage and burial registers can now be searched online at www.derry.rootsireland.ie.

Church registers of baptisms and marriages with their ability to build and confirm family links are the building blocks of family history. However, in terms of helping you trace 17th and 18th century ancestors they are frequently irrelevant owing to their non-existence. A summary of church registers in County Derry with pre-1800 baptism, marriage or burial entries is tabulated below.

There are no surviving Roman Catholic registers in County Derry prior to 1822. Fourteen Church of Ireland parishes (from 53) and three Presbyterian congregations (from 65) have baptism, marriage or burial registers predating 1800. This, therefore, means, that in most cases, there will be no surviving records of 18th century ancestors in church registers in Derry.
With one notable exception – St. Columb's Cathedral in Derry city – church registers are irrelevant to family historians seeking 17th century ancestors in County Derry.

## Pre-1800 Church Registers for County Derry

| Church | Baptisms | Marriages | Burials |
|---|---|---|---|
| **Church of Ireland** | | | |
| Arboe | 1775- | 1773- | 1776- |
| Coleraine | 1769- | 1769- | 1769- |
| Derryloran | 1795- | 1797- | 1797- |
| Desertlyn | 1797- | 1797- | 1798- |
| Desertmartin | 1752, 1785- | 1784- | 1783, 1788 |
| Drumachose | 1730-1752 | 1728-1753 | 1730-1736 |
| Dungiven | 1778- | 1778- | |
| Kilcronaghan | 1790- | 1748- | |
| Lissan | 1753-1795 | 1744-1794 | 1753-1795 |
| Maghera | 1785- | 1798- | |
| Magherafelt | 1718-1793, 1799- | 1720- | 1716-1771, 1799- |
| Tamlaghtard (Magilligan) | 1747-1768 | 1747-1753 | 1768-1775 |
| Tamlaght Finlagan | 1796- | 1796- | 1796- |
| Templemore (St. Columb's) | 1642- | 1649- | 1642- |
| **Presbyterian** | | | |
| Ballykelly | 1699-1709 | 1699-1740 | |
| 1st Garvagh | 1795- | 1795- | |
| 1st Magherafelt | 1703-1706, 1771-1780 | 1769-1782 | |
| **Moravian** | | | |
| Gracefield (Artrea) | 1750- | | |

The baptism, marriage and burial registers of St Columb's Cathedral, dating from 1642 to 1775, have been published and indexed in three volumes. Derry Central Library holds copies of these books, and Derry Genealogy Centre has indexed the pre-1864 baptism, marriage and burial registers of St. Columb's Cathedral.

## Gravestone Inscriptions

With civil registration of births and deaths commencing in 1864, and with the patchy survival of church records prior to 1820, gravestone inscriptions take on a special significance. Many Church of Ireland burial registers were destroyed in 1922, while the registers of the Roman Catholic and Presbyterian churches are especially poor regarding burial entries.

In many cases a gravestone inscription will be the only record of an ancestor's death. But gravestones offer much more than just the date of death; they frequently mention the townland address of the deceased together with the names, ages, and dates of death of other family members. Many graves are family plots and as a consequence list family members and their relationship to each other.

On identifying an ancestor's residence (i.e. townland or parish), the local graveyards should be visited. Church of Ireland graveyards should be examined irrespective of an ancestor's religion. Prior to the 1820s, owing to the operation of the Penal Laws, both Catholics and Presbyterians shared the same graveyards. And prior to the Burial Act of 1868, which permitted dissenting (i.e. Presbyterian) ministers to conduct burial services, the Church of Ireland clergy held jurisdiction over funeral services for all Protestants.

It is, unfortunately, true that the unkempt state of many graveyards (especially those now isolated from a functioning church) and the weathering of headstones precludes the reading of many inscriptions. It must also be said that only a small percentage of burials in any graveyard are marked by headstones.

Researchers should be aware that many old graveyards are now separated from a functioning church. With the establishment of new churches throughout the 19th century, many graveyards attached to the old church fell into disuse as new graveyards were opened beside a new church. The new church and graveyard were often located some distance away from the old church and graveyard.

The *Journal of the Association for the Preservation of the Memorials of the Dead,* over 47 years of its existence between 1888 and 1934, published more than 10,000 gravestone inscriptions collected from all over Ireland. A composite index to surnames and places for the first 20 years of publication was published in 1910. The National Library of Ireland holds a complete set of this Journal.

Derry Genealogy Centre has computerised headstone inscriptions from 114 graveyards in County Derry plus the pre-1930 registers of Derry City Cemetery. This database, which can be examined at www.derry.rootsireland.ie, will normally return the name of the graveyard, date of death, name of deceased, age and townland together with a comment recording relationships, where provided, to other people recorded on the same headstone.

**Wills**

Wills, by listing relatives – brothers, sisters, children and even grandchildren – are very valuable documents. It must be said that only a small proportion of the population – usually the better off, such as gentry, farmers and merchants – made wills.

Wills only take effect after the person dies and after they have been proved in court, i.e. a grant of probate has been issued. The grant of probate authenticates the will and gives the executors the power to administer the estate. Probate can take weeks, months or even years.

As well as wills you can come across 'letters of administration with will annexed' and 'letters of administration'. A grant of letters of administration with will annexed is issued where the executors were unable to carry out the terms of the will. If a person dies without making a will he is described as 'intestate'; in this case the court can grant 'letters of administration' (sometimes referred to as 'admons') which appoints administrators to administer the estate.

Although there is no guarantee that your ancestor made a will or, indeed, that a will has survived, as the bulk of Ireland's testamentary records (wills, administrations, probates, etc.) were lost in destruction of the Public Record Office of Ireland in 1922, I would recommend a search of any indexes that exist.

Before 1857, consistorial courts of the Church of Ireland, based in each diocese, were in charge of all testamentary affairs. Although most of these wills were destroyed in 1922 the indexes to these wills were not destroyed and they are available in the National Archives of Ireland. There was also a central Prerogative Court, under the authority of the Archbishop of Armagh as Primate of Ireland, which dealt with testamentary matters where the deceased's property was assessed to be worth more than £5 in more than one diocese.

Family Tree Maker's CD, *Irish Source Records*, includes *Indexes to Irish Wills, 1536-1857* and *Index to the Prerogative Wills of Ireland, 1536-1810.*

*Indexes to Irish Wills* is an alphabetical index of over 30,000 Diocesan wills proved in the Consistorial Courts of Ireland between 1536 and 1857. Arranged by Dioceses, and preceded by maps showing in which Dioceses the various Irish counties are situated, the *Indexes* provide the name of the testator, his parish, county, and the date of probate. The indexes to these pre-1858 church diocesan wills for Northern Ireland can also be searched, at no charge, by using the 'Name Search' option on the website of the Public Record Office of Northern Ireland at www.proni.gov.uk.

All of the Prerogative Wills of Ireland were destroyed by fire in Dublin in 1922, but before that Sir William Betham had made abstracts of the genealogical data in the wills from 1536 to 1800. In 1897 Sir Arthur Vicars prepared an index to Betham's abstracts, i.e. *Index to the Prerogative Wills of Ireland, 1536-1810.* This index has 40,000 entries arranged alphabetically by the name of the testator, showing his rank, occupation, or condition; his town or county of residence; and the year when the estate was probated.

The Irish Wills Index, containing over 102,000 names, to surviving testamentary records, which includes original documents, copies, transcripts, abstracts and extracts, held in the National Archives of Ireland (Dublin) for the time period 1484 to 1858 can be searched, by subscription, on the Irish Origins website at www.irishorigins.com. Each index entry contains the name of the person leaving a will, or being covered by a grant of probate or administration. It also contains their address, sometimes their occupation, and the place where the document was proved (i.e. a diocesan or the Prerogative court). The index also contains the names of the executors for almost half the entries, along with their addresses.

In January 1858 testamentary jurisdiction was transferred from Church control to the State. Thereafter all probates and administrations were granted at a principal registry in Dublin and eleven district registries. From 1858 to 1921, the Londonderry District Registry covered testators living in Counties Derry, Donegal and the baronies of Strabane and Omagh in County Tyrone.

Unfortunately the original wills of the Principal Registry up to 1904 and of the District Registries up to 1899 were lost in 1922 when the Public Record Office of Ireland in Dublin was destroyed. However, copy will books held by the District Registries survived as they had not been transferred to Dublin. The copy will books for Londonderry Registry District, prior to 1900, are now held in the Public Record Office of Northern Ireland.

From 1858, annual summaries of every grant of probate and letter of administration in Ireland were published, in alphabetical order by surname and first name of the deceased, in printed volumes called calendars. A complete set of these calendars for the whole of Ireland up to 1917 are held in both the National Archives of Ireland and the Public Record Office of Northern Ireland. The Probate Office at the Court House, Bishop Street, Derry also holds a complete set of the Calendar of Wills together with copy will books for Londonderry District Registry from 1900.

The Public Record Office of Northern Ireland is currently indexing and digitising all wills that were proved in the District Registries of Armagh, Belfast and Londonderry from 1858. A fully searchable index to the will calendars for these districts, from 1858 to 1965, can now be searched on their website, www.proni.gov.uk and, for the period 1858-1900, these are linked to digitised images of the wills themselves.

**1901 and 1911 Census Returns**

Although census enumerations were carried out every decade from 1821, the earliest surviving complete return for all Ireland is that of 1901.

The first four census enumerations, i.e. 1821, 1831, 1841 and 1851, were largely destroyed by fire in the Public Record Office at the Four Courts, Dublin in June 1922; and those for 1861, 1871, 1881 and 1891 were destroyed by government order.
In Ireland the census enumerations of 1901 and 1911 are open to the public. These returns were arranged by townland in rural areas and by street in urban areas.

The 1901 census records for each member of the household: their name, age, religion, education (i.e. if they could read or write), occupation, marital status, county or city of birth (or country, if born outside Ireland) and if a speaker of Irish. The 1911 census also provides additional information on the marriage; namely the number of years married, the number of children born and the number still living.

The 1901 and 1911 census returns should be examined once you have established where your ancestor lived at the turn of the 20th century.

The National Archives of Ireland holds the manuscript returns of the 1901 and 1911 censuses for all counties of Ireland. The Public Record Office of Northern Ireland holds microfilm copy of the 1901 census returns for the 6 counties of Northern Ireland. Derry Central Library holds microfilm copy of the 1901 and 1911 census returns for the city and county of Derry. Effective access to these census returns is through knowledge of the townland or street in which your ancestor lived. Without a name index it is impractical to search census returns for an ancestor if you hold no clues as to where they lived. A systematic search of census returns, on microfilm, townland by townland or street by street, requires much patience.

The computerisation, however, of both the 1901 and 1911 census returns for Derry changes this; it is now straightforward to search these sources by name as well as by place.

The National Archives of Ireland in association with Library and Archives Canada have digitised the 1901 and 1911 census returns for all counties of Ireland. All name, age and place information has been indexed and linked to digital images of the actual 1901 and 1911 census returns; 4,500 reels of microfilm containing 6 million images were digitised. This means that, in addition to being able to search the 1901 and 1911 returns by both name and place, you can now view, at no charge, an image of the original household census form for any named individual at www.census.nationalarchives.ie. This means that it is feasible to search 1901 and 1911 census returns for a named individual with little or no knowledge of where they lived in the city or county of Derry.

Census of Ireland on the night of SUNDAY, the 31st of MARCH 1901

Mill Street, Londonderry

No. on Form B. 39

| Name and Surname | Relation to Head of Family | Religious Profession | Education | Age | Sex | Rank, Profession or Occupation | Marriage | Where Born | Irish Language |
|---|---|---|---|---|---|---|---|---|---|
| James Candy | Head of Family | Catholic | Read & Write | 42 | M | Railway Station Master | Married | Coleraine | |
| Mary C Candy | Wife | Catholic | Read & Write | 40 | F | Wife | Married | Portrush | |
| Margaret A Candy | Daughter | Catholic | Read & Write | 12 | F | Scholar | Not married | Ballymena | Irish & English |
| Mary M Candy | Daughter | Catholic | Read & Write | 11 | F | Scholar | Not married | Belfast | Irish & English |
| Thomas J Candy | Son | Catholic | Read & Write | 9 | M | Scholar | Not married | Londonderry City | |
| Anna Madeline Candy | Daughter | Catholic | Read & Write | 7 | F | Scholar | Not married | Londonderry City | |
| Joseph Phelan Candy | Son | Catholic | Read & Write | 5 | M | Scholar | Not married | Londonderry City | |
| Elizabeth G Candy | Daughter | Catholic | Cannot read | 4 | F | Not yet at school | Not married | Londonderry City | |
| James R Candy | Son | Catholic | Cannot read | 2 | M | Not yet at school | Not married | Londonderry City | |

The database of Derry Genealogy Centre, at www.derry.rootsireland.ie, contains a partial transcription, detailing names and residences, of all people recorded in the 1901 census returns for the city and county of Derry.

## Mid-19th century Griffith's Valuation

In Ireland, the almost total loss of the census returns of 1821, 1831, 1841 and 1851 and the complete destruction of the census returns of 1861, 1871, 1881 and 1891 means that sources which act as 19th century census substitutes are very important to Irish family history researchers.

One such source is Griffith's Primary Valuation. Griffith's Valuation, or Primary Valuation of Ireland, was carried out between 1848 and 1864, under the direction of Sir Richard Griffith, to determine the amount of rates each household should pay towards the support of the poor within their poor law union. Each poor law union was named after a chief town in the district, and usually serviced the area in a ten-mile radius, often extending across county boundaries. In detailing every head of household and occupier of land in Ireland, against a townland address in rural areas or street address in urban areas, Griffith's Valuation is viewed as a census substitute for post-Famine Ireland.

This source details against every property in mid-19th century Ireland: the occupier's name; the landlord's name; description of property; size of farm (if applicable); and rateable valuation of any buildings and land. The results of the survey were published in volumes by poor law union. Hence, the Valuation for County Derry was printed in five books; with the poor law union books for Ballymoney, Londonderry and Newtownlimavady being published in 1858, and those for Coleraine and Magherafelt in 1859. Copies of these Valuation Books are widely available in local libraries and national record offices.

**GRIFFITH'S VALUATION**

| Townland | **COOLNAMONAN** |
|---|---|
| Parish | **BANAGHER** |
| Barony | **TIRKEERAN** |
| Poor Law Union | **NEWTOWNLIMAVADY** |
| County | **LONDONDERRY** |
| Publication Date | **1858** |
| Ordnance Survey Map Number | 30 |
| No. and Letters of Reference to Map | 16      13*h* |
| Occupier | **Michael Hassan (*Roe*)** |
| Immediate Lessor | **Trustees Robert Ogilby** |
| Description of Tenement | House, offices, & land |
| Area (16) | 18 acres 0 roods 39 perches |
| Area (13h) | 0 acres 0 roods 25 perches |
| Rateable Annual Valuation of Land (16) | £10 -   0 shillings - 0 pennies |
| Rateable Annual Valuation of Land (13h) | £0 -   2 shillings - 0 pennies |
| Rateable Annual Valuation of Buildings (13h) | £1 -   8 shillings - 0 pennies |
| Total Annual Valuation of Rateable Property | £11 - 10 shillings - 0 pennies |

At first glance the family historian might feel disappointed with Griffith's Valuation as it names heads of household only. With no information provided on family members within each household or relationships between householders it is not possible to confirm the nature of linkages between named people in this source.

Griffith's Valuation, however, can deliver much valuable insight into the economic and social status of an ancestor as it measures farm size and details valuations of land and buildings. It, furthermore, can assist in locating the ancestral home and in identifying what type of settlement an ancestor lived (for example in an isolated farmstead, village or town).

A very significant feature of Griffith's Valuation was the compilation of maps to accompany the survey. Every lot number in Griffith's Valuation (recorded under the heading "No. and Letters of Reference to Map") was marked on a copy of the Ordnance Survey map (at a scale of 6 inches to 1 mile). This effectively means that the locations of all properties in the mid-19th century - houses and farms - can be identified once you have found your ancestor in Griffith's Valuation. In other words with these maps you can identify with accuracy the location of the ancestral home (even if it is long gone) or farm. Copies of these Griffith's Valuation or Second Valuation maps for County Derry are held in Coleraine Library, Mellon Centre for Migration Studies and Public Record Office of Northern Ireland.

An examination of Griffith's Valuation and their associated maps for County Derry confirms that in many rural areas, and in particular in marginal areas less suited to economic farming, the population was still living in small village clusters that had not yet been broken up into the dispersed farm dwellings which dominate the Irish landscape today. Such clusters of farmhouses in "farm towns" without church, shop or public house were called clachans.

Clachans were associated with a communal system of farming known as rundale, where farms consisted of infield and outfield sections and where agriculture was subservient to the demands of cattle herding. The bonds of kinship were close and strong among the occupants of clachans with new houses being added as holdings were subdivided among co-heirs. Furthermore, clachans were associated with the townland unit, the smallest and most ancient of Irish land divisions. Indeed clachans, at one time, were the nuclei of Ireland's network of townlands.

For example, of 21 householders recorded in Griffith's Valuation in the townland of Coolnamonan, Banagher parish, five miles southwest of the town of Dungiven, 12 of them, including 8 Hassan families, were living in a clachan, also named Coolnamonan, and farming 42 fields scattered in and around their settlement and all located within the townland of Coolnamonan.

Griffith's Valuation map is reproduced here, highlighting the land farmed by Hassan families who were all living in a clachan, marked as number 13 on the map and named as Coolnamonan.

Another interesting feature of Griffith's Valuation is the use of nicknames to distinguish one household of the same name from another in the same townland.

Griffith's Valuation clearly confirms the dominance of the surname Hassan in Coolnamonan. In Coolnamonan at this time there were three households headed by James Hassan and two by Michael Hassan, as comments in italics were added in brackets after their names. These comments may have referred to the first name of their father, to their occupation or to a nickname associated with that particular family.

# HASSAN FARMS IN COOLNAMONAN
## 1858

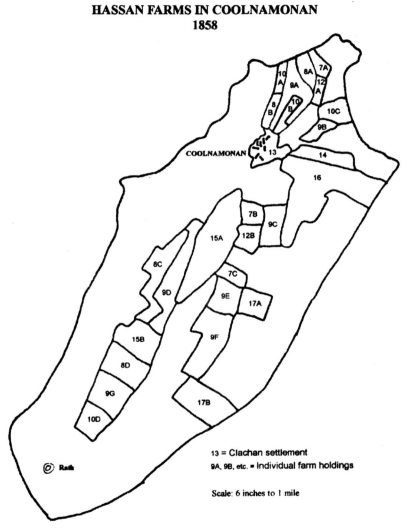

13 = Clachan settlement

9A, 9B, etc. = Individual farm holdings

Scale: 6 inches to 1 mile

Source: GRIFFITH'S VALUATION

**Hassan Households in Coolnamonan in 1858**

| Head of Household | Map Reference | Details of Property |
|---|---|---|
| James Hassan *(Jonny)* | 7 | House, offices & land |
| James Hassan *(Tonry Due)* | 8 | House, offices & land |
| John Hassan | 8ca | House |
| Patrick Hassan | 9 | House, offices & land |
| Thomas Hassan | 10 | House, offices & land |
| Michael Hassan *(Jack Roe)* | 12 | House, offices & land |
| Nelus Hasson | 13 | House and garden |
| Alick Hassan | 14 | Land |
| John Hassan | 15 | House, offices & land |
| Michael Hassan *(Roe)* | 16 | House, offices & land |
| James Hassan *(Tailor)* | 17 | House, offices & land |

Nicknames, in particular, are priceless pieces of information to have when you visit the local area and talk to local people. For example, in Coolnamonan, the only effective way to distinguish one Hassan family from another is by their nicknames. Thus knowing, for example, that you are related to the *Jack Roe* Hassans could be all-important. It might even unlock a door to oral tradition, predating any church registers, which has been passed down through succeeding generations.

You can now search, for free, the mid-19<sup>th</sup> century Griffith's Valuation at www.askaboutireland.ie/griffith-valuation by Family Name and Place Name. 'Family Name Search' provides transcript details, the original document page and appropriate Valuation map for any selected occupier. Use the 'Place Name Search' option to find everyone who lived in a particular place.

Family Tree Maker has published in CD, *An Index to Griffith's Valuation of Ireland, 1848-1864*, which names more than one million Irish householders against their county, parish and townland of residence. This index includes 34,546 records for County Derry. The database of Derry Genealogy Centre at www.derry.rootsireland.ie also contains an index to Griffith's Valuation entries for County Derry, as does Dr. William Macafee's CD, *Researching Derry & Londonderry Ancestors: A practical guide for the family and local historian*, and website at www.billmacafee.com.

You can also access, at no charge, an online index to Griffith's Valuation by searching 'Ancestry Library Edition', at any branch library in Northern Ireland, on the Northern Ireland Library Service's website www.librariesni.org.uk.

## Early-19th century Tithe Applotment Books

Owing to the destruction of most early-19th century census returns the Tithe Applotment Books are widely used by family history researchers as a census substitute for pre-Famine rural Ireland.

The Tithe Applotment Books were compiled between 1823 and 1837, by civil parish, and they list all landholders, against their townland address, who paid tithe. Tithe was a tax, based on land valuation which was determined by farm size and quality of land; it was paid by all landholders, irrespective of religious denomination, for the support of the Established Church (i.e. Church of Ireland).

Tithe Books, therefore, will record the names of tenant farmers but not of urban dwellers or landless labourers. A landholder may also appear more than once on a list, thereby indicating that they held more than one piece of land. The results of this assessment were published in hand-written volumes by parish. Copies of these Tithe Books are available in the Public Record Office of Northern Ireland.

This source usually details against every landholder in early-19th century Ireland: the landholder's name; size of farm (in acres, roods and perches); quality of land (1st class, 2nd, 3rd etc.); valuation of land; and amount of tithe composition (in pounds £, shillings s, and pennies d).

Tithe Books, like Griffith's Valuation, name heads of household only; it doesn't name any other family members. However, in addition to confirming the ancestral home (i.e. townland) of an ancestor, the tithe entry of a landholder, by variously detailing farm size, quality and valuation of land, and amount of tithe to be paid, will offer some insight into the economic and social status of an ancestor.

In Tithe Books land is measured in acres, roods and perches. As a generalisation, there were 40 perches to a rood and 4 roods to an acre. Different land measurements have been used in Irish land surveys since the 17th century. In Tithe Books land was usually measured in Irish Plantation acres and in the mid-19th century Griffith's Valuation in English acres or Statute acres. The 'Irish' or 'plantation' acre was equal to 1.62 'statute' or 'English' acres. An Irish acre is, therefore, bigger than an English acre. Thus, 5 'Irish' acres were equivalent to 8 'English' or 'Statute' acres. In Ulster, in particular, land could also be measured in 'Scottish' acres. The 'Cunningham' or 'Scottish' acre was equal to 1.29 statute acres. Thus, 5 'Irish' acres are equivalent to 6.45 'Scottish' acres. Researchers, therefore, need to be aware of these differences when comparing farm sizes in different surveys.

Regarding valuations in Tithe Books there were 12 pennies (d) to a shilling (s) and 20 shillings to a pound (£). Decimalisation was introduced in 1970.

Family Tree Maker has published in CD, *Tithe Applotment Books, 1823-1838*, an index to some 200,000 landholders extracted from the Tithe Books of 233 parishes in the six counties of Northern Ireland. Landholders are listed by surname and forename against their townland, parish and county of residence. Derry Genealogy Centre has also indexed Tithe entries for County Derry which you can examine by searching 'Census Substitutes for Co. Derry' at www.derry.rootsireland.ie and selecting 'Early 19th Century Tithe Books' as the source.

You can access an online index, for free, to 200,000 Tithe Applotment entries of the 1820s and 1830s for Counties Antrim, Armagh, Derry, Down, Fermanagh and Tyrone by searching 'Ancestry Library Edition', at any branch library in Northern Ireland, on the Northern Ireland Library Service's website www.librariesni.org.uk.

## 1831 Census

The first four census enumerations of Ireland, i.e. 1821, 1831, 1841 and 1851, were largely destroyed by fire in the Public Record Office at the Four Courts, Dublin in June 1922; and any surviving fragments of these census returns are held in the National Archives of Ireland, Dublin with microfilm copies in the Public Record Office of Northern Ireland, Belfast.

County Derry is fortunate in that an abstract of the 1831 census has survived. This census, arranged by parish and townland, lists: the name of each head of household; the number of individual families in each house; the number of males and females, including servants, in each household; and their religious denomination. Although this source lists the names of all heads of households, over 40,000 in total, in County Derry it doesn't name the other family members within each household.

In County Derry alone the 1831 census complements and, indeed, provides additional information to that recorded in the Tithe Applotment Books.

Unlike the Tithe Books, which is in effect a census of rural inhabitants, the 1831 census names all heads of households, rural and urban, in County Derry. The 1831 census, by locating families by townland in rural areas and by street in urban areas, can confirm the ancestral home of all of Derry's inhabitants. Furthermore, by identifying the religious denomination of all households it will guide researchers in selecting appropriate church registers to search for baptism, marriage and burial details.

**1831 CENSUS**

| Townland | **BALLYGODEN** |
|---|---|
| Parish | **FAUGHANVALE** |
| Barony | **TIRKEERAN** |
| County | **LONDONDERRY** |
| Name of Owner or Occupier | **Edward Cain** |
| Number of House | 13 |
| Number of Families in each | 2 |
| Number of Males in Family | 1 |
| Number of Females in Family | 1 |
| Number of Male Servants | -- |
| Number of Female Servants | -- |
| Religion | Roman Catholic |

Derry Genealogy Centre has indexed 1831 census entries for County Derry which you can examine by searching 'Census Substitutes for Co. Derry' at www.derry.rootsireland.ie and selecting '1831 Census' as the source. Dr. William Macafee in his CD, *Researching Derry & Londonderry Ancestors: A practical guide for the family and local historian*, and website at www.billmacafee.com, has also indexed the 1831 census.

Pension search summaries can act as a partial reconstruction of 1841 and 1851 census returns. The Old Age Pension Act was introduced in 1908. For persons applying to the local Pensions Officer for a pension with no proof of age (i.e. that they were over 70 years old) searches were requested of the 1841 and 1851 censuses at the Public Record Office, Dublin. These searches were all completed before the fire in 1922.

The Old Age Pension search summaries for the Republic of Ireland are held in the National Archives of Ireland and for Northern Ireland in the Public Record Office of Northern Ireland.

Indexes to these Old Age Pension search summaries have been published as *Ireland: 1841/1851 Census Abstracts (Northern Ireland)* and *Ireland: 1841/1851 Census Abstracts (Republic of Ireland)* in Family Tree Maker's CD, *Irish Source Records*. Although only a small fraction of the population is covered by these summary book abstracts, these Pension search summaries, by salvaging some census data of 1841 and 1851, identify 23,000 individuals in Northern Ireland and 5,800 persons in the Republic of Ireland.

**Pre-1800 Census Substitutes**

In terms of tracing 17th and 18th century ancestors in County Derry the most realistic strategy is to examine the wide range of pre-1800 census returns and census substitutes, usually compiled by civil parish, that survive, for any references to a surname of interest. Transcripts and copies of many of these sources can be found in the Public Record Office of Northern Ireland.

From a family historian's point of view it is disappointing that these census returns and census substitutes name heads of household only. As no information is provided on family members within each household or relationships between householders it is not possible to confirm the nature of linkages between named people in these sources.

Census substitutes, however, are very useful in confirming the presence of a family name in a particular townland and/or parish, and in providing some insight into the frequency and distribution of surnames. These sources, for example, can prove very illuminating in highlighting the spread of English and Scottish settlers into County Derry.

Surnames can provide much useful insight, if not proof, of family origins in Ireland. In 17th century Derry most surnames can tentatively be identified as being English, Scottish or Irish in origin.

The most useful pre-1800 census substitutes for County Derry are as follows:

### Flax Growers' Lists of 1796

In 1796 the Irish Linen Board published a list of almost 60,000 individuals, by county and parish, who had received awards for planting flax, the raw material of linen. This was, in effect, especially in Ulster where the linen industry was strong, a census of rural Ireland at the end of the 18th century. This source names 5,106 flax growers in County Derry.

Family Tree Maker has published in CD, *Irish Flax Growers List, 1796*, which names 60,000 flax growers (from all counties in Ireland except Dublin and Wicklow) and the civil parish and county in which the flax was grown.

### Religious Census of 1766

Compiled by Church of Ireland rectors, in 1766, these returns listing heads of household, showing their religion, as between Church of Ireland (Episcopalian), Roman Catholic (termed 'Papists' in the returns) and Presbyterian (or Dissenters), survive for ten parishes in County Derry (i.e. Artrea, Ballynascreen, Banagher, Bovevagh, Derryloran, Desertlyn, Desertmartin, Drumachose, Dungiven and Magherafelt). This source identifies 3,233 inhabitants of County Derry; in some returns only their parish address is provided, while in others the townland address is given.

## Protestant Householders' Lists of 1740

These lists of Protestant heads of household, compiled in 1740 by county, barony and parish, survive for all County Derry parishes. This source names 8,646 residents of County Derry; in some cases only their parish address is provided, while in others the townland address is given.

## Hearth Money Rolls of 1663

This tax of 2 shillings, raised for every hearth or fireplace, was introduced in 1662. The roll for County Derry, giving the name and amount each head of household had to pay against their townland, town (and street in Derry city) and parish address, was compiled in 1663. This source names 2,789 taxpayers in County Derry.

## Muster Rolls

Throughout the 17th century, landlords mustered their tenants periodically to identify adult males capable of military service. Muster Rolls, listing names, usually by estate, were compiled in County Derry in 1622, 1630 and 1642. Most of the names in these rolls are of Planter or British origin, although a few native Irish names are also recorded.

The Muster Roll of 1622 names 290 'British Men' in the City and Liberties of Londonderry (110), the Town and Liberties of Coleraine (100), and the Vintners' estate at Bellaghy (80).

The Muster Roll of 1630 is by far the most extensive for the county. It names 1931 'British Men' (1605 of whom lived on the estates of the London Companies) who resided on 19 estates in County Derry; only two estates, the Salters' Company and Skinners' Company, provided no muster lists.

The 'Muster rolls of foot companies in the garrison of Londonderry', dated May 1642-August 1643, names 905 foot soldiers, organised into 9 companies, who defended Derry's walls during the siege of 1641/42. These men would have been drawn from estates throughout County Derry.

It is clear that the walled city of Londonderry was of crucial importance to the establishment of a strong plantation in north-west Ireland. By May 1628, 265 houses had been built inside the walls and leased to 155 families. These details are all recorded in a Rent Roll dated 15 May 1628 which was published, by the Londonderry Sentinel in 1936, as *A Particular of the Howses and Famylyes in London Derry May 15, 1628*. Derry Central Library holds a copy of this book.

The Siege of Derry, which lasted 105 days from April 1689, was a by-product of the struggle for the English throne between James II, who had the support of Louis XIV of France, and William of Orange with the backing of the English Parliament. Researchers seeking ancestors in Derry during the Siege of Derry should examine *Fighters of Derry Their Deeds and Descendants* by William R Young (published 1932) which names 1660 "Defenders" and 352 officers of the "Jacobite Army". Derry Central Library holds a copy of this book.

Indexes to many of these pre-1800 census substitutes are contained in two databases; namely, 'Census Substitutes' database at www.derry.rootsireland.ie, and in Dr. William Macafee's CD, *Researching Derry & Londonderry Ancestors: A practical guide for the family and local historian,* and website at www.billmacafee.com.

The indexes to a number of databases of 18th century census returns and census substitutes for Northern Ireland,  such as the1740 Protestant Householders Lists, 1766 Religious Census Returns and Dissenters petitions of 1775 (Dissenters refers to Protestants who were not members of the Church of Ireland, i.e. Presbyterians etc), can also be searched, at no charge, by using the 'Name Search' option on the website of the Public Record Office of Northern Ireland at www.proni.gov.uk.

## Local Record Offices

### Local libraries

There are two libraries, in particular, that hold family history sources of county-wide significance; namely Derry Central Library and Coleraine Library. Contact details, opening hours and summary description of sources held in these two libraries are listed in this section.

Derry, furthermore, is well served by a network of local libraries throughout the county. They will hold material of interest to local and family historians. Contact details and opening hours for these libraries – in towns such as Draperstown, Dungiven, Garvagh, Kilrea, Limavady, Maghera, Magherafelt and Portstewart – can be found on the website of the Northern Ireland Library Service at www.librariesni.org.uk.

All library members in Northern Ireland have access, by internet, for free, at their local library to an extensive range of databases provided by Ancestry.com. With more than 7 billion names and 26,000 searchable databases, Ancestry.com (www.ancestry.com) claims to be the number one online source for family history information with the web's largest collection of historical records.

At your local library you simply log onto the Library Service's website (i.e. www.librariesni.org.uk), select the 'Online Library' option and then 'Ancestry Library Edition'. You then gain access to very significant databases such as US Census Returns from 1790 to 1930, US Immigration Collection of ship passenger lists and UK Census Returns from 1841 to 1901. Furthermore, it provides local family history researchers with the opportunity to search the indexes to a wide range of Irish sources, which includes:

- Griffith's Valuation of 1848-1864

- Tithe Applotment Books of 1824-1837
- Flax Growers Lists of 1796
- 1766 Religious Census fragments naming 11,000 heads of households
- 'Irish Records Extraction Database' containing 100,000 names with details of births, marriages, deaths, census entries, wills and immigration data, dating from 1600 to 1874, extracted from 120 sources.
- Royal Irish Constabulary records from 1816 to 1921
- Irish Immigrant arrivals at New York, with 600,000 entries, between 1846 and 1851
- Irish Diocesan Wills from 1536 to 1858
- Database of Irish Marriages 1771-1812 as found in Walker's *Hibernian Magazine*

This resource is only available from the Libraries NI network; you can't access, for example, the 'Ancestry Library Edition' from your computer at home.

**Derry Central Library**
35 Foyle Street
Derry
County Londonderry
BT48 6AL
Telephone: +44 28 7127 2310
Email: derrycentral.library@librariesni.org.uk

Opening Hours:       Monday and Thursday 8.30am to 8pm
                     Tuesday, Wednesday and Friday 8.30am to 5.30pm
                     Saturday 9.30am to 4.30pm

This library holds an extensive family history collection which includes: 1901 and 1911 census returns (on microfilm) for the city and county of Derry; Griffith's Valuation Book for poor law union of Londonderry; Newspapers (on microfilm) – *Derry Journal* 1825 to present, *Derry Standard* 1836 to 1964,

*Londonderry Sentinel* 1829 to present and *Belfast Newsletter* 1752 to 1925; Town Directories 1820 to 1870 (trade directories for towns throughout County Derry); and *Derry Almanac and Directory* 1871 to 1953, with gaps (household lists, by Street, for Derry city).

Publications of interest in its extensive collection include:

- *Londonderry and The London Companies 1609-1629* by Sir Thomas Phillips (published 1928) contains muster rolls of the inhabitants of the City of Londonderry and Town of Coleraine in 1622. It also contains illustrations of the estates, towns and villages of the London Companies in 1622.
- *A Particular of the Howses and Famylyes in London Derry May 15, 1628* (published 1936) names 155 tenants inside walls of Londonderry in 1628.
- *Fighters of Derry Their Deeds and Descendants* by William R Young (published 1932) names 1660 "Defenders" and 352 officers of the "Jacobite Army" at the Siege of Derry of 1689.
- Published, and indexed, in three volumes – 1642-1703, 1703-1732 and 1732-1775 – the baptismal, marriage and burial registers of St. Columb's Cathedral, Derry city.
- *The Londonderry Sentinel: Births, Marriages and Deaths 1829 - 1869*. This CD details 6,800 births, 9,900 marriages and 18,700 deaths published in the *Sentinel* between 1829 and 1869.
- Index to all households in Derry city, with street address and house number, as recorded in *Derry Almanac and Directory* of 1874 and 1901.
- Four books of passenger lists, with index, detailing County Derry emigrants: *Irish Passenger Lists, 1803 – 1806; Passengers from Ireland, Lists of Passengers Arriving at American Ports Between 1811 and 1817; Irish Emigration Lists, 1833 – 1839; and Irish Passenger Lists, 1847 – 1871.*

- *Ordnance Survey Memoirs of Ireland: Index of People and Places*. This index provides access to over 100,000 references to people and places recorded in the Ordnance Survey Memoirs. The memoirs, compiled in the 1830s, provide a detailed and unique insight into life in all of Derry's parishes prior to the Famine. The Memoirs for County Derry have been published in 14 volumes which are available in Derry Central Library.

**Coleraine Library**
Queen Street
Coleraine
County Londonderry
BT52 1BE
Telephone: +44 28 7034 2561
Email: coleraine.library@librariesni.org.uk

Opening Hours:
Monday and Wednesday 9.30am to 8pm
Tuesday and Thursday 9.30am to 6pm
Friday and Saturday 9.30am to 5pm
Sunday 1pm to 5pm

This library holds an extensive family history collection which includes: Church registers (on microfilm) of all denominations for Coleraine, Derry, Limavady and Magherafelt district council areas; Griffith's Valuation Books for poor law unions of Ballymoney, Coleraine and Magherafelt; Griffith's Valuation maps; 1740 Protestant Householders Lists; 1796 Flax Growers Lists; and Newspapers (on microfilm) - *Coleraine Chronicle* 1844 to present, *Coleraine Constitution* 1877 to present, and *Coleraine Herald* 1897 to 1902.

The Library also has a copy of the following book: *The Coleraine Chronicle: Births, Marriages and Deaths 1844 -1869 and The Ballymoney Herald: Births, Marriages and Deaths 1860 - 1863*. Published by Coleraine Branch of North of Ireland Family History Society (www.nifhs.org) this publication (which can be purchased on CD) identifies 3,660 births, 5,900 marriages and 8,890 deaths.

**The Mellon Centre for Migration Studies**
Ulster American Folk Park
2 Mellon Road
Castletown
Omagh
County Tyrone
BT78 5QY
Telephone: +44 28 8225 6315
Website: www.qub.ac.uk/cms
Email: mcms@librariesni.org.uk

Opening Hours:          Tuesday to Friday 10.30am to 4.30pm
                        Saturday 10.00am to 4.00pm

The Mellon Centre for Migration Studies has built up the Irish Emigration Database (accessible online at www.dippam.ac.uk), which contains many passenger lists, mainly for the period 1800 to 1860. Their library also holds: Griffith's Valuation (on microfiche) for the nine counties of Ulster; First and Second (i.e. Griffith's) Valuation Maps for six counties of Northern Ireland; Newspapers (on microfilm) - *Derry Journal*, with gaps, from 1772 to 1887; and Street and Town Directories dating from 1846 to 1920.

**Foyle Family History Centre**
The Church of Jesus Christ of Latter-day Saints
Racecourse Road
Londonderry
BT48 7RE
Telephone:  +44 28 7135 0179
Email: foylefhc@gmail.com

Opening Hours:          Monday: 10am to 4pm,
                        Wednesday: 2pm to 9pm
                        Friday: 10am to 4pm

Foyle Family History Centre holds on microfilm copies of the following civil registers for all Ireland: Births from 1864 to 1881 (first quarter); Marriages 1845 to1870; and Deaths 1864 to 1870. There is no charge for using their facilities. As there are a limited number of microfilm readers it is advisable to book in advance by telephone.

**Archive and Genealogy Service**
Heritage and Museum Service
Derry City Council
Foyle Valley Railway Museum
Foyle Road
Derry
BT48 6SQ
Telephone: +44 28 7126 5234
Website: www.derrycity.gov.uk/Museums
Email: bernadette.walsh@derrycity.gov.uk

Opening Hours:　　　Monday to Friday 10am to 4pm

The main group of Council records are minute books, letter-books and correspondence, legal documents, architectural drawings, maps and plans and a limited photographic collection. The Heritage and Museum Service also acquire and preserve private collections. This material ranges from entire business archives, literary collections, military items, railway and maritime collections and political documents. Public access to the archive collection is by appointment.

The minute books of Londonderry Corporation from 1673 to 1901 have been digitised and can be accessed at www.proni.gov.uk.

The database of Derry Genealogy Centre, at www.derry.rootsireland.ie, contains the bulk of pre-1922 civil birth and marriage registers for the city and county of Derry, the early baptismal and marriage registers of 85 churches, gravestone inscriptions from 117 graveyards, and census substitutes and census returns dating from 1663 to 1901.

Visitors and locals alike are welcome, at no charge, to forward any queries they may have concerning their family history to the genealogist, Brian Mitchell, who has been involved in local, family and emigration research in the wider Derry area since 1982; by contacting him, by email, at genealogy@derrycity.gov.uk.

**The Major Record Offices**

**General Register Office**, Government Offices, Convent Road, Roscommon, Ireland
Telephone: +353 90663 2900
Website: www.groireland.ie
Email: gro@groireland.ie

The General Register Office also maintains a family history research facility for the purpose of searching indexes to birth, death and marriage records and for obtaining photocopies of records indentified from the indexes at Werburgh Street, Dublin 2.

Research Room: Open Monday to Friday 9.15 am to 4.45 pm.

Sources:
Births and deaths registered in whole of Ireland from 1 January 1864 to 31 December 1921. Marriages registered in whole of Ireland from 1 April 1845 to 31 December 1921. Births, marriages and deaths for Ireland (excluding Northern Ireland) from 1 January 1922.

Fees:
A particular search of indexes for 5 years €2.00
A general search of indexes for 1 day covering all years €20.00
A photocopy of an identified entry €4.00

**General Register Office Northern Ireland (GRONI)**, Oxford House, 49-55 Chichester Street, Belfast, BT1 4HL, Northern Ireland
Telephone: +44 28 9151 3101
Website: www.nidirect.gov.uk/gro
Email: gro.nisra@dfpni.gov.uk

Research Room: Open Monday to Friday 9.30 am to 4.00 pm (The indexes are computerised. As there are limited spaces in the search room it is advisable to book by telephone or email)

Sources:
Birth and death registers for the six counties of Northern Ireland from 1st January 1864 to the present-day and civil marriage registers for Northern Ireland from 1st April 1845 to the present-day.

Fees:
Computerised indexes can be searched for 6 hours at cost of £14.00. This cost includes 2 verifications of entries by staff with the option of further verifications at £4.00 each.
Assisted search of records with member of staff at £35 per hour.

The General Register Office of Northern Ireland is committed to making its historical registers of births (i.e. records over 100 years old), marriages (over 75 years old) and deaths (over 50 years old) accessible online. As of 31 March 2014, by purchasing credits (one credit costs £0.40) to search and view records, GRONI online went live.

**National Archives of Ireland,** Bishop Street, Dublin 8, Ireland
Telephone: +353 1407 2300
Website: www.nationalarchives.ie
Email: mail@nationalarchives.ie

Opening Hours: Monday to Friday 9.15 am to 5.00 pm

Sources:
This office's collection is very extensive and of all-Ireland significance. It holds wills; microfilm copies of many pre-1870 Church of Ireland registers (original registers will be held locally or in Representative Church Body Library in Braemor Park, Churchtown, Dublin 14; email, library@ireland.anglican.org); 1901 and 1911 census returns; Griffith's Valuation; Tithe Books; surviving 19$^{th}$ century census returns and Religious Census of 1766.

The National Archives provides a Genealogy Advisory Service where members of the public can consult a professional genealogist about sources relating to their family history. It is free and open to the public Monday to Friday from 10.00 am to 1.30 pm.

The National Archives of Ireland in association with Library and Archives Canada have digitised the 1901 and 1911 census returns for all counties of Ireland. This means that, in addition to being able to search the 1901 and 1911 returns by both name and place, you can now view, at no charge, an image of the original household census form for any named individual at www.census.nationalarchives.ie.

**National Library of Ireland,** Kildare Street, Dublin 2, Ireland
Telephone: +353 1603 0200
Website: www.nli.ie
Email: info@nli.ie

Opening Hours:        Monday to Wednesday 9.30 am
to 7.45 pm
Thursday to Friday 9.30 am to 4.45 pm
Saturday 9.30 am to 12.45 pm

Sources:
Microfilm copies of the registers of most Roman Catholic parishes in Ireland for years up to 1880 and of the early-19th century Tithe Applotment Books. The National Library also holds on microfiche the mid-19th century Griffith's Valuation. In addition the library holds a comprehensive collection of directories, photographs, newspapers, maps and manuscripts.

The National Library also offers a free Genealogy Advisory Service as an ideal starting point for those beginning family history research No appointment is necessary.

Opening Hours:        Monday to Wednesday 9.30 am
to 5.00 pm
Thursday to Friday 9.30 am to 4.45 pm

**Public Record Office of Northern Ireland (PRONI)**, 2 Titanic Boulevard, Titanic Quarter, Belfast, BT3 9HQ, Northern Ireland
Telephone: +44 28 9053 4800
Website: www.proni.gov.uk
Email: proni@dcalni.gov.uk

Opening Hours:  Monday, Tuesday, Wednesday and Friday
9.00 am to 4.45 pm
Thursday 10.00 am to 8.45 pm

Sources:
This office's collection relates mainly to the nine counties of the province of Ulster (i.e. Counties Antrim, Armagh, Down, Fermanagh, Londonderry and Tyrone in Northern Ireland and Counties Cavan, Donegal and Monaghan in the Republic of Ireland). It holds wills; microfilm copies of most church registers of all religious denominations; microfilm copy of 1901 census returns (for Northern Ireland only); Griffith's Valuation; Griffith's Valuation maps (for Northern Ireland only); Tithe Books; and surviving 19th century census returns.

The Public Record Office of Northern Ireland (PRONI) is committed to making its archives more widely available. You can now search online their eCatalogue to locate over one million catalogue entries relating to PRONI's archives.

Furthermore, PRONI have created a number of significant online databases to records, with Northern Ireland-wide coverage, in their collection, such as: Street Directories 1819 to 1900: Will Calendars 1858 to 1965 (which, for the period 1858 to 1900, are linked to digitised images of the wills themselves); pre-1840 Freeholders' Records of Registers and Poll Books (which lists people entitled to vote, or people who voted, at elections); and Ulster Covenant (which identifies just under half a million original signatures and addresses of men and women who signed the Ulster Covenant on 28 September 1912). You can now also search online, via their 'Name Search' option, indexes to pre-1858 wills, 1740 Protestant Householders Lists and Religious Census of 1766.

CPSIA information can be obtained at www.ICGtesting.com
Printed in the USA
LVOW09s0358040215

425546LV00012B/159/P